35 DAYS
35 WAYS

DELICIOUS RECIPES FOR THE VEGAN LIFESTYLE

Printed in the United States of America

First Printing, 2018

Creative Direction: Shamara Elle
Book Cover Design: Kayo Williams
Cover Photo: Kayo Williams
Editor: Takitta Ollison
Food Photography: Juan Benavides
Stylist: Juan Benavides
Published by Still Standing Publishing Co.

ISBN 9781791314217

PROLOGUE

35 Days, 35 Ways was inspired at the age of 35. I believe if people repeat the same thing for 30 days it becomes a habit and success will follow. Typically, most habits are broken at least once within a continuous 30-day pattern. Reverting to familiarity is common when incorporating changes into our daily routine. The first day transitioning to vegan, I was accustomed to not looking at labels. I didn't pay attention to the dairy in ranch dressing or the croutons used in my salad until it was pointed out to me! The first 30 days were challenging; I needed an additional five days on standby for the comfort of possible slip-ups. I begin to think if people had a 35 day guide help plan weekly and monthly meals, a grocery list, or an understanding of vegan meal prep, lives would change drastically. My vegan journey began July 2017. It wasn't as difficult as I assumed, mostly because I considered the vegetarian lifestyle a few years ago, but I felt it was more difficult to find a variety of fruits and vegetables like it is presently. In addition, I had already eliminated all meat except chicken, turkey, and seafood. Personally, I was ready for change; my body needed it. The more I researched health alternatives, I realized I was not properly educated on alternative inexpensive healthy food options, and the truth of how certain foods are made shocked me. I had no idea how inexpensive my grocery list was about to become, or the broad selections of fruits and vegetables present in local markets. The inspiration to create this guide came after getting several recipe requests from friends, and the best part is watching my non-vegan friends enjoying the dishes I prepare! My goal is to inspire others who desire to make long term diet changes but are clueless like I was about how to prepare simple delicious vegan meals with items stored in your pantry.

I would like to thank God for opening doors and placing everyone in my life during this journey to make my dreams reality. There is always a great team behind each success. My team is full of love and support and too many to name individually. To my Mom, Brenda Sawyer, thank you for always believing in me, praying for me, and teaching me how to cook at an early age. To Adrian Sawyer, my brother, and the first sampler, thanks for giving my food a try when my mom was unable to cook for us; trusting my skills!! I appreciate your technology skills adding to the value this cookbook. Thank you to my late great-grandmother Catherine Midgette who passed down so many culinary gifts and talents; she was an awesome cook, seamstress, and much more; I am Her! Thank you to my late great Grandfather Mr. Stilley who instilled in me this entrepreneurial spirit; he owned a small store back home in Vandemere, NC. He was also my first example of an entrepreneur. To Victor Castillo, my Gusband, who has always had my back no matter what I pursued and always eager to taste test my dishes, I thank you! To my publisher Tamiko Lowry-Pugh, thank you for taking on this challenge, encouraging me, and supporting me through the process. Finally, to my friends, family, supporters, etc., without your love none of this would be possible, I appreciate and love you all! I pray this not only changes your life but blesses your soul!

Shamara Elle

CONTENTS

FREQUENTLY ASKED QUESTIONS

Q: Are you really Vegan?

A: Yes, I am really vegan! Most people are shocked to learn I prepare delicious food and eat a variety of different vegetables and food. I understand solely consuming vegetables and fruit is uncommon, this allow me to educate people on the vast variety of options and creative ways to recreate your favorite recipe vegan style.

Q: What is Vegan?

A: Veg*an /ˈvēgən/ n. - a person who does not eat or use animal products.

Adj. - using or containing no animal products.

Q: What do you eat?

A: I eat a variety of vegetables and fruits. I had no idea of the broad options available until I became vegan. It's refreshing to get away from the traditional sources of meat protein. My favorite food is avocado, and I love to prepare is guacamole; I'm addicted!

Q: What do you eat for protein?

A: I eat a variety of beans: kidney, red, black, white, black eye peas, lentils, great northern, chickpeas, chia seeds, hemp seeds, almond, etc.

Q: Why did you decide to go vegan?

A: For years I wanted to become vegetarian but then the options were few and not as broad as today. After watching the documentary, "What the Health" myself and a friend decided to remove meat from our diets and consume only vegetables and fruits.

Q: Do you miss meat or get cravings?

A: I don't miss meat unless I leave my house unprepared or have not eaten. I learned quickly the key to a consistent vegan lifestyle is to prepare meals ahead of time and create a grocery list.

Q: What did you struggle with in the beginning?

A: In the beginning, I struggled with meal preparation! If I left my house unprepared, no snacks didn't eat anything or enough to keep me full for a few hours I would crave everything non-vegan. I learned to prep my food and plans my days efficiently when I have errands to run. It's easier to remain focused.

Q: Do you have energy?

A: Yes, I have so much more energy. Prior to my diet change, after each meal I would immediately get sleepy. Work days after lunch were a struggle for me. Now, after I eat a meal, I feel light, energized, and full of life! I am living my BEST LIFE!!!!

BEVERAGES, SMOOTHIE BOWLS & SMOOTHIES

The first time I made this water, I used strawberries; the strawberry version was my favorite until one day I got creative with my ingredients! Searching the fridge, I noticed a container with leftover fresh pineapple, which also had juice sitting at the bottom (the best). With no strawberries in sight, I improvised and made use of what I had available. Voila, "Pineapple Lemon Gingerade" was born! It's refreshing, cool, and just the right mix of ginger and pineapple. I have made the pineapple and strawberry version for my friends. Pineapple always seems to be the winner! The strawberry version is delicious as well; please try it or use any fruit you like; I've also added mango.

Pineapple Lemon Gingerade

Ingredients

- **2 tbsp agave**
- **½ gal water**
- **½ pineapple peeled and sliced**
- **¼ c grated ginger**
- **½ lemon juiced**

Instructions

1. Fill a large container with water.
2. Add lemon juice, ginger, and ½ of the sliced pineapple.
3. Mix well; add agave.
4. Refrigerate for at least 3-6 hours.
5. Reuse ingredients the next day, then discard.

You may substitute pineapple for strawberry, mango, watermelon, etc. The possibilities are endless and either way the water is delicious.

Cucumber Lemon Lime Water

Ingredients

- ½ gallon water
- ½ lime, sliced
- ½ lime juiced
- ½ cucumber, sliced
- ½ lemon sliced
- ½ lemon juiced
- Handful of mint leaves

Instructions

1. Combine all ingredients in a pitcher.
2. Allow the ingredients to chill in the refrigerator for at least four hours before serving.
3. Drink throughout the day or discard after 48 hours.

Hot Chocolate

Ingredients

- 2 c dairy free milk
- 2 tsp vanilla essence or scrapings from 1 vanilla bean
- 4 tbsp brown sugar
- 1 cinnamon stick or 1 tbsp cinnamon
- 1 tbsp chocolate shavings
- 3-4 pods star anise
- 4 tbsp unsweetened cocoa powder or dark chocolate

Instructions

1. In a medium saucepan, pour 1-2 cups of water over high heat bring star anise and cinnamon to a boil. Use more water for thinner hot chocolate.
2. Add cocoa and cover pan. Boil for 15 minutes on medium low heat, until the cocoa has dissolved with the water. Remove from heat.
3. Pour through a strainer or sifter, discard solids, and return mixture to

pan.

4. Turn mixture to lowest setting. Stir in non-dairy milk and vanilla. Add cane sugar or maple syrup. Simmer 10-20 minutes.

5. Enjoy hot with whole wheat or grain toast. Dip bread in chocolate for a flavor bomb!

SMOOTHIE BOWLS

Peanut Butter Chocolate Blitz Bowl

Ingredients

- **2 bananas (frozen)**
- **1 Sliced banana (unfrozen)**
- **2 tbsp nuts**
- **1 tbsp peanut butter**
- **1 tbsp cocoa powder**
- **1 c milk**
- **⅓ c vegan chocolate chips**

Instructions

1. Add frozen bananas and all ingredients into blender.
2. Add additional milk to desired consistency.
3. Pour in bowl. Garnish with sliced unfrozen banana, cocoa powder, and chopped nuts.

Tropical Fruit Smoothie Bowl

Ingredients

- 1 tbsp agave
- 1 c vegan milk
- ¼ c pomegranate seeds
- ¼ c papaya
- ¼ c mango
- ¼ c guava
- ½ tsp chia seeds

Instructions

1. Place all ingredients in blender until smooth.
2. Add additional milk and agave according to desired thickness and consistency.
3. Pour in bowl. Garnish with mango, pomegranate, guava, papaya, nuts, and chia seeds.

SMOOTHIE

Green Smoothie

Ingredients

- 2 kiwis sliced
- 1 c pineapple gingerade (pg. 3)
- 1 frozen or fresh banana
- ½ c frozen spinach
- ½ c vegan milk
- ½ c frozen kale
- ½ tsp grated ginger (optional)
- 2 tbsp cucumber diced
- 1 tbsp hemp seeds

Instructions

1. Place all ingredients in blender until smooth.
2. Add additional gingerade and agave according to desired thickness and consistency.

Berry Beauteous Smoothie

Ingredients

- **1 c vegan milk or ginger pineapple lemon gingerade (pg. 3)**
- **1 tbsp blackberries**
- **1 tsp beets diced**

- **1 tbsp agave**
- **1 c strawberries**
- **¼ c blueberries**
- **¼ c raspberries**

Instructions

1. Place all ingredients in blender until smooth.
2. Add additional water and agave according to desired thickness and consistency.

BREAKFAST

WAFFLES

Prep Time: 10-15 minutes

Cook Time: 10-20 minutes

Hot Waffle Iron! The pan must be very hot for waffles to come out right. If you add the batter into a mildly-warm pan, they will stick to the iron. Turn the setting to about three notches from max setting. If you don't hear a sizzle the moment the batter hits the pan, redo that batch. Let the waffle cook completely; if you attempt to remove while batter is not done it will stick. It is normal for the waffle iron to smoke as it cooks.

Keep them warm and fresh. When making large batches of waffles for family and friends, it can be challenging keeping them all warm since you can only make one at a time. I keep mine warm in the toaster oven by turning to the lowest oven setting. Conventional oven: Add a cooling rack to the oven and warm oven to the lowest temperature setting possible, not to exceed 200º F.

Ingredients

- **2 c All-Purpose unbleached flour**
- **1 tsp apple cider vinegar**
- **1 tsp vanilla bean or extract**
- **1 tsp corn starch**
- **1 tsp backing powder**
- **1 ¼ c cane sugar**
- **1 c vegan milk (add more or less to desired consistency)**
- **½ c of milk (buttermilk)**
- **⅛ tsp cinnamon**
- **¼ tsp cardamom**

Berry Compote

Ingredients

- ½ c blueberries
- ½ c strawberries
- ½ c cane sugar
- 1 tbsp freshly squeezed lemon juice

Instructions

1. In a medium bowl mix berries, sugar, and lemon juice. Set aside.

2. Heat waffle iron on high heat, about one notch down from the highest setting. Preheat oven to lowest setting.

3. Mix berries, ¼ cup of sugar, and lemon juice and let soak while batter is prepared.

4. Mix vanilla, apple cider vinegar, and ½ cup milk. Set aside for 5 to10 minutes (this will cause milk to curate and create buttermilk).

5. In a medium bowl, whisk flour, cinnamon, cardamom, baking powder, sugar, and cornstarch.

6. Add "buttermilk" to dry ingredients, mix well. Add remaining milk and stir until well combined. Be careful not to over mix. Tiny lumps may remain.

7. Pour batter into the heated waffle iron, enough to cover the center and most of the central surface area. Cook for 4 to 5 minutes or until iron has stopped steaming and the waffle is deeply golden. If waffle sticks, continue cooking an additional 2 to 3 minutes before checking again. When you can lift entire waffle from skillet easily, it is done.

8. Transfer it to a cooling rack or baking sheet. Don't stack your waffles on

top of each other, or they'll lose crispness. Place in oven to keep warm. Repeat for more!

9. Garnish waffles with berry compote, maple.

Roasted Red Potatoes

Prep Time: 25-30 minutes

Cook Time: 25-35 minutes

Ingredients

- **5-6 medium red potatoes**
- **1 Vidalia onion**
- **1 green pepper**
- **1 red pepper**
- **1 yellow pepper**
- **1 orange pepper**
- **4 garlic cloves diced**
- **2 tbsp avocado oil**
- **2 tbsp smoked paprika**
- **2 tbsp paprika**
- **1 tsp saffron**
- **1 tsp turmeric**
- **2 tbsp seasoning salt or all-purpose seasoning**
- **¼ tsp cayenne pepper**

Instructions

1. Preheat oven to 350°F.
2. Wash potatoes. Cut into medium size dice shape pieces. Rinse again and pat dry with paper towel.
3. Heat avocado oil in a medium size cast iron skillet. As oil heats, add smoked paprika cook for a minute; add paprika. I prefer a little char on my potatoes (be sure oil is extremely hot to achieve this). Cook 10 minutes before stirring.
4. Turn heat to medium low add onions, peppers, all-purpose seasoning, salt, black pepper, and cayenne pepper and cook for 10 minutes.
5. Place skillet in oven for 10-15 minutes or until potatoes are golden brown and soft. Add more seasoning if desired.

Roasted Acorn Squash Boats

Prep Time: 10-15 minutes

Cook Time: 20-30 minutes

Ingredients

- **1 small acorn squash**
- **1 banana sliced**
- **dash cardamom**
- **¼ tsp cardamom**
- **⅛ tsp cinnamon**
- **½ tsp avocado oil**
- **¼ c strawberry**
- **¼ c blueberry**

Instructions

1. Preheat oven to 400°F.
2. Wash outside of squash and cut in half. Remove all seeds from squash. Rinse squash and seeds. I like to roast the seeds and enjoy later.
3. Sprinkle cinnamon, cardamom, and drizzle olive oil.
4. Lay flat and cook for 20 to 30 minutes or until tender.
5. Let squash cool for 5 to10 minutes.
6. Add yogurt, fruit, nuts, and drizzle with maple syrup.

Yellow Corn Grits (with tomatoes and spinach)

Prep Time: 10-15 minutes

Cook Time: 20-30 minutes

Grits

Ingredients

- **2 c grits**
- **1 c water**
- **1 tbsp vegan butter**
- **½ c vegan milk**
- **¼ tsp salt**
- **⅛ tsp pepper**

Instructions

1. In a medium pot bring water to a boil, add milk, grits, and butter. Turn heat to low. Cover and cook 30 minutes stirring occasionally. Add more milk until desired consistency is achieved.
2. Place in a bowl, top with sautéed spinach and tomato.

Spinach and Tomato

Ingredients

- **4 c spinach**
- **1 c tomatoes**
- **1 tbsp avocado oil**
- **¼ tsp salt**
- **¼ black pepper**
- **4 garlic cloves**
- **2 tbsp diced onion**

Instructions

1. In a skillet on medium heat, pour avocado oil. Add spinach, tomatoes, salt, and pepper. Cook until spinach is tender.

Overnight Breakfast Jars

Prep Time: 10-15 minutes

Banana Pudding

Ingredients

- 1 16 oz mason jar
- 1 c rolled oats
- ½ c vegan milk (I prefer unsweetened almond)
- 1 sliced banana
- 1 tbsp maple syrup
- ½ tsp vanilla extract
- ¼ tsp cinnamon
- dash cardamom

Instructions

1. Place lid on jar and sit in fridge overnight.
2. When ready to eat, add more milk if oats are too dry.
3. I like to add a drizzle of maple syrup.

Raspberry Chocolate Chia Pudding

Ingredients

- 1 16 oz mason jar
- ¼ c chia seeds
- 1 c diced raspberries
- ½ c vegan milk
- ½ c vegan mini chocolate chips
- 1 tsp vanilla extract or scrapings from vanilla bean
- 2 tbsp coconut cream
- 1 tbsp cocoa powder

Instructions

1. Add the ingredients in mason jar. Stir to combine. Place this in the refrigerator to chill for at least 3 hours or overnight.
2. Remove from refrigerator after chilling and chia seeds have absorbed the liquid. Add more almond milk for desired consistency.
3. Top with strawberries and vegan chocolate chips. Serve and enjoy!

Blueberry Delight

Prep Time: 10-15 minutes

Ingredients

- 1 16 oz mason jar
- 1 c rolled oats
- ½ c vegan milk (I prefer un-sweetened almond)
- 1 c blueberries
- 1 tbsp maple syrup
- ½ tsp vanilla extract
- 1 tbsp lemon juice
- ¼ c vegan sweetened yogurt

Instructions

1. Place lid on jar and sit in fridge overnight.

2. When ready to eat, add more milk if oats are too dry.

3. Top with yogurt and blueberries.

4. I like to add a drizzle of maple syrup.

Breakfast Toast Spreads

Prep Time: 0-5 minutes

Cook Time: 5-7 minutes

Banana Peanut Butter & Banana

Ingredients

- 2 tbsp peanut butter
- 1 sliced banana
- 2 tbsp vegan chocolate chips
- ½ tsp cocoa powder (garnish)
- ½ tbsp chia seeds

Instructions

1. Toast bread.

2. Spread peanut butter (nut butter of choice).

3. Add sliced banana, chocolate chips, and chia seeds.

4. Drizzle with cocoa powder.

Spinach Mushroom Avocado Toast

Prep Time: 5-10 minutes

Cook Time: 0-5 minutes

Ingredients

- 2 avocados
- 2 c fresh spinach
- 1 tomato
- 1 tbsp cilantro
- 1 tbsp red onion

- 1 tbsp avocado oil
- ½ tbsp jalapenos diced
- ⅛ tsp salt
- ⅛ tsp pepper

Instructions

See Appetizers for guacamole recipe.

1. Heat avocado oil in medium skillet. Add mushrooms, garlic, and thyme. Sauté for 5 minutes or until mushrooms soften.
2. Add Spinach, sauté for two three minutes.
3. Toast bread until golden brown.
4. Spread a layer of guacamole, top with sauté mushrooms and spinach.

Strawberry Chia Jam (with pistachios)

Prep Time: 5-10 minutes

Cook Time: 5-7 minutes

Ingredients

- **2 ½ c diced strawberries**
- **1 tsp coconut cream**
- **¼ c maple syrup (optional)**
- **2 tbsp Chia Seeds**
- **Water as needed**

Instructions

1. Place diced strawberries, chia seeds, coconut cream, and maple syrup (if using) into a blender. Blend on medium to high speed until preferred jam consistency is obtained. Add water 1 tbsp at a time as needed to liquify mix.
2. Pour contents of blender into a small saucepan and heat over medium heat until the jam begins to bubble. Reduce heat to low and simmer for 5-7 minutes, or until the jam starts to thicken.
3. Remove from heat and immediately pour into a mason jar. Allow to cool completely and then store in the fridge for up to one week.

Toast:

Instructions

1. Toast bread to desired setting.
2. Spread strawberry chia jam and sprinkle with pistachios (nuts of choice).

APPETIZERS

For a guacamole lover such as myself, avocados are a girl's best friend. I may be bias, but I feel hands down I have the best guacamole ever. The interesting thing is, I learned from a good friend, then I made a few adjustments I'd refer to as the Shamara touch. Whenever I make guacamole it's one of the first dishes gone. One of my friends says I never make enough! I could eat guacamole every day.

Guacamole

Prep Time: 5-10 minutes

Prep Time: 15 minutes

Ingredients

- 4 Avocados
- 2 tbsp cilantros
- 1 tbsp adobo seasoning
- ½ tsp jalapeño
- ½ lime juice
- ½ red onion
- ¼ tsp salt
- ¼ tsp pepper

Instructions

1. In a mixing bowl, spoon avocados and lime juice. Get avocados as smooth as possible.
2. Add cilantro, diced onion, salt, pepper, adobo, onion, jalapeño, lime, and cilantro. Stir together well.

Cauliflower Bites

Prep Time: 5-7 minutes

Cook Time: 25-30 minutes

Ingredients

- **1 head of cauliflower**
- **1 tbsp black pepper**
- **1 tbsp garlic powder**
- **1 tsp paprika**
- **2 c cooking oil (vegetable,)**
- **½ tsp sea salt**
- **½ black pepper**
- **½ c vegan breadcrumbs**
- **½ c unbleached all-purpose flour**
- **¼ c cornstarch**
- **¼ c vegan milk**
- **¼ c rolled oats**

Instructions

1. Heat oil in medium sized frying pan on medium heat.
2. Cut and wash head of cauliflower. Gently pat with paper towel removing all excess water.
3. Mix cauliflower in a bowl with all seasonings and milk.
4. Add flour and cornstarch. Add more for thicker consistency. Set aside.
5. Coat with breadcrumbs and oats and drop in hot oil.
6. Cook until golden brown. Remove from oil and place on paper towels to drain oil.Coat with desired sauce and bake for 15 minutes at 350ºF.
7. Dip in sauce and enjoy.

I prefer to season cauliflower overnight or at least six hours prior to cooking.

See sauces (pg. 82): BBQ, Lemon Pepper

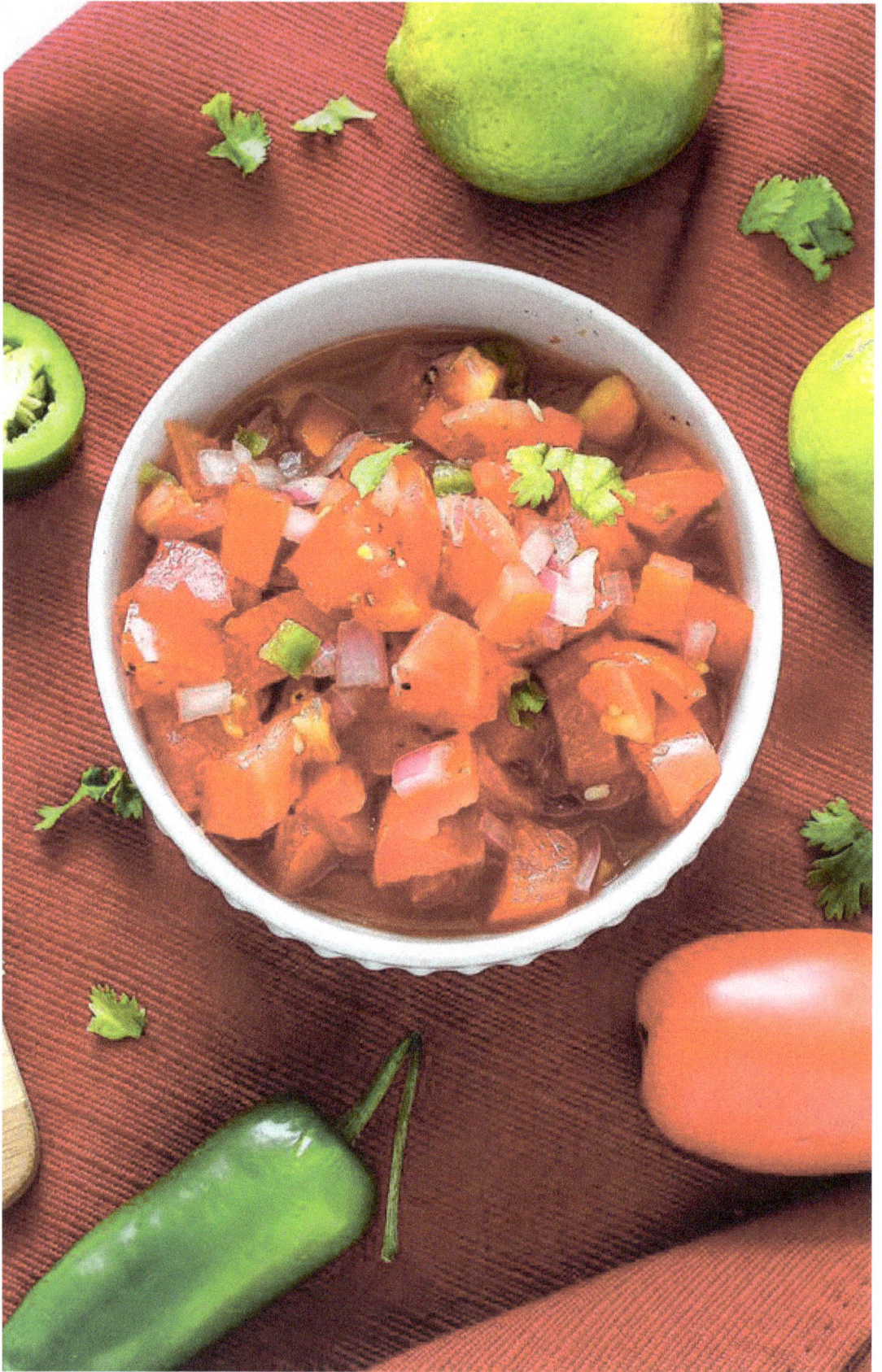

Pico De Gallo

Prep Time: 10-15 minutes

Completion Time: 5 minutes

Ingredients

- **4 tomatoes diced**
- **1 pinch salt**
- **1 pinch pepper**
- **1 tsp jalapeño diced**
- **½ red onion diced**
- **½ lime juice**
- **4 tbsp cilantro**
- **1 tbsp all-purpose seasoning**

Instructions

1. Dice tomatoes, add salt, pepper, lime juice, onion, garlic, and jala-peños. Stir ingredients.
2. Add mango or pineapple to Pico.

Serve with dipping chips and enjoy.

Sweet Potato Chips

Prep Time: 25-30 minutes

Cook Time: 120 minutes

Ingredients

- **2 large sweet potatoes**
- **1 tbsp cinnamon**
- **dash cayenne pepper**
- **1 tbsp grapeseed oil**
- **1 tsp sea salt**

Instructions

1. Preheat oven to 250°F.

2. Wash and slice the potatoes into one fourth inch pieces using a medallion. You may use a knife; pieces may not cut evenly.

3. Wash the potatoes and pat gently with a paper towel be sure the potatoes are dry.

4. Line baking sheet with parchment paper.

5. Lay the dried potatoes on the parchment (keep them as spaced as possible). Season with cinnamon, cayenne pepper, and salt. Drizzle with olive oil and mix around the sheet. Spread them back apart.

6. Bake an hour, turn the chips over and bake for another hour.

7. Make sure chips are spread apart to achieve an even cook and crispy taste.

Zucchini-Squash Bake

Prep Time: 10-15 minutes

Cook Time: 15-20 minutes

Ingredients

- **2 zucchinis**
- **2 squash**
- **½ Vidalia onion**
- **2 tomatoes**
- **1 tsp saffron**
- **½ tsp cumin**
- **1 tsp turmeric**
- **1 tbsp oregano**
- **1 tbsp parsley**
- **½ juice of lemon**
- **2 garlic cloves**
- **1 pinch of salt**
- **1 pinch of pepper**
- **1 tbsp of grapeseed oil**

Instructions

1. Preheat oven to 400°F.
2. Dice veggies into ¼ inch pieces and place in a glass baking pan; sprinkle all seasonings throughout except parsley and lemon juice. Add oil evenly.
3. Bake for 15-25 mins or until veggies are cooked to preference.
4. Remove from oven, and squeeze lemon juice evenly over veggies.
5. Garnish with parsley.

Potato Fries

Prep Time: 5- 10 minutes

Cook Time: 10-15 minutes

Ingredients

- **4 medium potatoes**
- **2-3 c of oil (vegetable)**
- **1 tbsp. old bay seasoning**
- **1 tbsp. parsley**

Instructions

1. Cut potatoes 1-inch slices or use a vegetable medallion.
2. Soak in a bowl of water for at least 30 minutes to remove excess starch.
3. Drain very well and pat dry with paper towels.
4. In a medium pot, heat oil over medium heat.
5. Cook 10-15 minutes or until crispy.
6. Season with parsley, all-purpose seasoning, and old bay.
7. Serve with Sriracha aioli (pg. 81).

SOUPS & SALADS

Vegetable Broth

Prep Time: 30-45 minutes

Cook Time: 60-90 minutes

Crockpot: 6-8 hours

Ingredients

- 1 chopped celery stalk
- 1 carrot
- 4 garlic cloves
- 2 celery stalks
- 1 tomato
- ½ c zucchini
- ½ c yellow squash
- ½ c kale
- 1 c spinach
- ¼ c beets
- ½ c mushrooms
- ½ c turnip
- 1 vidalia onion sliced
- ½ c red onion sliced
- 1 jalapeño whole (uncut)
- 1 red pepper sliced
- 1 green pepper sliced
- 1 yellow pepper sliced
- 1 orange pepper sliced
- 2 tbsp thyme
- 1 bay leaf
- 2 tbsp parsley
- 2 tbsp cilantro
- 1 tsp black pepper
- 1 tsp coconut oil
- 2 tbsp oregano
- ½ tbsp garlic powder
- ½ tsp onion powder
- 1 tbsp turmeric
- 1 tbsp saffron
- ⅛ tsp cumin
- ⅛ tsp sea salt
- 1 tsp black pepper
- 1 tsp coriander
- ½ tsp red pepper flakes
- 1 vegetable bouillon cube
- ½ tsp Better Than Bouillon vegetable base

Instructions

1. In a large pot, heat grapeseed oil. Add onion, grated garlic, red onion, scallions, and cilantro, then cook for 5 minutes.
2. Add chopped carrots and thyme; sauté 15 minutes. Add 3 cups of water and boil for 30 minutes.
3. Strain vegetables from liquid.

Crockpot:

1. Fill Crockpot with water and add all vegetables and seasoning.
2. Cook on high for at least three hours then reduce to low heat and cook an additional four to six hours.
3. Strain vegetables from liquid.
4. Store in mason jars and freeze.

I use all leftover scraps of vegetable to make broth. Simply freeze in a sandwich bag and add veggies as you cut them.

Another useful tip is to sit your herbs: parsley, thyme, etc., out to dry and use them when needed.

Butternut Squash Chili

Prep Time: 10-20 minutes

Cook Time: 45-60 minutes

Crockpot: 6-8 hours

Ingredients

- 1 c red kidney beans
- 1 c black beans
- 1 can of Zesty Chili diced tomatoes
- 1 small to medium butternut squash
- 1 tsp jalapeño pepper diced (seeds removed)
- 1 green pepper diced
- 1 yellow pepper diced
- 1 orange pepper diced
- ½ vidalia onion diced
- 4 garlic cloves
- 4 c of vegetable broth
- 1 tbsp grapeseed oil
- 1 tbsp tomato paste
- 1 tsp red pepper flakes
- ½ tsp cumin
- ½ tsp black pepper
- 2 tsp chili powder
- 2 tbsp paprika
- 2 tbsp smoked paprika
- 2 tbsp chili powder
- 2 tbsp southwest chili blend seasoning
- 1 pinch of salt

Instructions

1. Cut butternut squash in medium size squares. Wash, rinse, and let dry.

2. In a medium pot heat grapeseed oil; add onion, grated garlic, and peppers for about two minutes we do not want to overcook the peppers.

3. Stir in butternut squash, cumin, black pepper, salt, paprika, and chili powder. Sauté 15 minutes.

4. Add vegetable broth, beans, diced tomatoes, jalapeño pepper, tomato paste, and chili powder. Gently stir incorporating all the ingredients

5. Cover and let cook on medium heat for 30-45 minutes.

6. Serve with vegan sour cream, vegan cheese, and crackers. Garnish with cilantro and lime.

Crockpot:

1. Fill Crockpot with water and add all ingredients.

2. Cook on high for at least four hours then reduce to low heat and cook an additional 2-4 hours.

Lentil Soup

Prep Time: 10-20 minutes

Cook Time: 45-60 minutes

Crockpot: 6-8 hours

Ingredients

- **2 c lentils (washed and soaked over-night or at least 4 hours)**
- **3 c vegetable broth**
- **1 c water**
- **3 diced tomatoes**
- **2 chopped carrots**
- **1 tbsp olive oil**
- **1 tbsp tomato paste**
- **1 tbsp scallions**
- **1 chopped celery stalk**
- **4 garlic cloves**
- **1 tsp thyme**
- **1 tsp cilantro**
- **1 tsp black pepper**
- **1 pinch of sea salt**

Instructions

1. In a pot heat olive oil, add onion, grated garlic, red onion, scallions, cilantro, and complete seasoning. Cook for 5 minutes.
2. Add chopped carrots and sauté for 10 minutes.
3. Pour in vegetable broth and tomato paste simmer on medium high 15 minutes.
4. Drain soaked lentils and add to broth. Boil for 45 minutes. For a thicker consistency of soup add more tomato paste and a tbsp. of non-diary milk
5. Check texture of beans. Depending on softness one may need to boil for up to additional 15 minutes.
6. Serve with toast or crackers!

Crockpot:

- Fill Crockpot with water and add all ingredients.
- Cook on high for at least four hours then reduce to low heat and cook an additional 2-4 hours.

Potato and Leek Soup

Prep Time: 30-45 minutes

Cook Time: 60-90 minutes

Crockpot: 6-8 hours

Ingredients

- 4 Russet potatoes
- 4 garlic cloves
- ½ c vegan milk
- 4 c vegetable broth
- 1 leek diced
- ½ vidalia onion
- 1 tbsp grapeseed oil
- 1 pinch salt
- ½ tbsp vegan butter
- 1 tsp pepper
- 1 tbsp garlic and herb seasoning

Instructions

1. Wash and cut potatoes into medium diced sized pieces. Slice leek into one-inch pieces.
2. Heat grapeseed oil in a medium pot. Add potatoes, garlic, garlic and herb seasoning, pepper, salt, leek, and butter. Sauté for 15 minutes.
3. Add vegetable broth and cover. Cook for 15 mins or until potatoes are tender.

4. Add milk . Cover and cook for 15 mins or until potatoes are tender.

Crockpot:

1. Fill Crockpot with water and add all vegetables and seasoning.
2. Cook on high for at least 4 hours then reduce to low heat, cook 4-8 hours.

Mushroom-Onion Pho

Prep Time: 20-35 minutes

Cook Time: 30-45 minutes

Crockpot: 2-4 hours

Ingredients

- 4 c vegetable broth
- 2 c mushroom (your choice)
- 2-4 whole star anise
- 1 onion julienne
- 4 garlic cloves
- 1 carrot julienne
- 1 yellow pepper
- 1 green onion
- 1 red pepper
- 2 whole coves
- 2 tbsp coconut amino or low sodium soy sauce
- 2 tbsp sesame oil
- 2 c rice noodles

For Topping

- Lime wedges
- Coconut amino
- Jalapeno sliced
- 2 tbsp scallions
- 1 bunch mint
- Fresh basil
- Chili oil
- Sriracha sauce

Instructions

1. Pour vegetable broth into a large pot and place over high heat. Bring to a simmer.

2. While broth heats up, heat sesame oil on low in a wok. Sauté peppers, ginger, and garlic. Watch carefully to avoid burning vegetables.

3. Add onion and ginger to broth along with cinnamon, star anise, cloves, and coconut amino. Simmer for at least minutes.

4. While broth simmers cook noodles based according to package direction. Drain into a colander and rinse with cold water. Set aside.

5. When broth has simmered for at least 30 minutes drain to remove onion, ginger, and spices. Return broth to pot add mushrooms, simmer for about 5 minutes. Add carrots and simmer for about a minute until tender.

6. Place noodles in bowl, add broth and veggies over top. Garnish with toppings.

Crockpot:

1. Fill Crockpot with water and add all vegetables and seasoning.

2. Cook on high for 3 hours then reduce to low heat and cook for 1 hour.

*I*n life there are always subtle reminders of our favorite childhood dishes whether it was prepared by our mother, sister, or auntie. Regardless the age we expect every version to resemble the taste of a loved one. My mother's potato salad is the only potato salad I eat other than mine, of course. Whenever I prepare this dish it's all eaten and recipe request start rolling in. I was nervous about making this dish vegan, although the only ingredient I left out are the eggs; however, for some it is the most important. Momma's potato salad does not disappoint and omitting one ingredient doesn't damage the overall dish. This is my mother's version. Feel free to recreate your loved one's recipe.

Momma's Potato Salad

Prep Time: 10-15 minutes

Cook Time: 10-20 minutes

Ingredients

- **4 russet potatoes**
- **4 cups of water**
- **1 tbsp celery stalk or celery seeds**
- **4 tbsp vidalia onion**
- **2 tbsp yellow mustard**
- **4 tbsp green pepper**
- **½ c vegan mayo**
- **⅛ tsp of salt**
- • **⅛ tsp pepper**

Instructions

1. Wash potatoes and cut into medium diced size pieces. Rinse once more and drain all excess water.

2. In a medium pot boil about 4 cups of water. Add potatoes when water begins to boil. Cook on medium high for 10-15 minutes or until tender.

3. Rinse potatoes with cold water and drain very well. Transfer to mixing bowl.

4. Add potatoes, mayo, mustard, chopped celery, diced onion, salt, and pepper. Stir all ingredients together until you have a nice light, yellow color. You may need to add more mustard according to taste.

5. Cover with plastic wrap and place in fridge for 1-2 hours before eating.

Green Goddess Salad

Prep Time: 15-25 minutes

Ingredients

- 1 avocado
- 1 c kale
- 2 c spinach
- 2 c arugula
- 1 c spring mix

- ½ c cucumbers
- 1 c tomatoes
- ½ c shredded carrots
- ½ c dried cranberries
- ½ c unsalted pecans
- ½ c golden raisins

Instructions

1. In a medium bowl mix kale, spinach, arugula, spring mix, cucumbers, carrots, dried cranberries, and pecans.

2. Cut tomatoes and place in a separate bowl (the water from tomatoes makes veggies soggy).

3. Pour dressing and lightly toss to evenly distribute.

4. Place in serving bowl and enjoy.

*See Sauces (pg. 82)

Fruit Bomb Platter

Although fruit is the healthiest food to eat for breakfast, I seriously believe this platter is all about the color and vibrance of the presentation. Most people eat with their eyes first. Meaning if the food looks pretty, delicious, or inviting, most will try it. This Bomb Platter is not only aesthetically pleasing to the eye but is packed with healthy sugars and energy in its natural form. You can substitute with any fruit you desire, just be sure to add some exotic fruit. People will want to eat this because of the unique variety of fruit.

Prep Time: 15-20 minutes

Ingredients

- 1 c strawberries diced
- 1 c blueberries
- 1 pineapple diced
- 1 c mango diced
- 1 c raspberries
- 1 c nectarines
- 1 c grapes (seeded)
- 1 c papaya diced

- 2 bananas
- 2 orange or tangerine peeled
- 2 red apples sliced
- 2 granny smith apples sliced
- 2 kiwis sliced
- 2 dragon fruit diced
- ½ c plums sliced
- 1 handful lychee peeled

Instructions

1. Dice fruit into ½ inch pieces and place in medium bowl.

2. Place in fridge to chill or enjoy immediately.

Toppings, depending what you like and have handy:

- plain yogurt

- honey

- grated dark chocolate

- grated coconut

- nuts

Asparagus Salad

Prep Time: 5-10 minutes

Cook Time: 5 minutes

Ingredients

- **1 bunch of asparagus**
- **½ c of cherry tomato**
- **1 tbsp grapeseed oil**
- **2 cloves garlic**
- **1 tbsp unsalted walnuts**
- **1 tbsp balsamic vinegar**

Instructions

1. In a medium skillet heat oil.

2. Add asparagus, salt, garlic, and pepper. Sauté for 2 minutes.

3. Add cherry tomatoes, balsamic vinegar, and walnuts. Sauté for 1 minute.

Chickpea "Tuna" Salad

Prep Time: 15-20 minutes

Ingredients

- **1 - 15 oz. can or 1 cup chickpeas**
- **2 tbsp finely chopped onion**
- **1 tbsp green onion**
- **⅓ c vegan mayonnaise**
- **½ tsp lemon juice**
- **½ tsp old bay seasoning**
- **¼ tsp celery seeds or fresh diced celery**
- **dash sea salt**
- **1 tsp garlic powder**
- **dash ground pepper**

Instructions

1. Drain and rinse the chickpeas. Mash them in a bowl with a potato masher or fork.

2. Add the remaining ingredients and combine well. Store in the fridge for up to 5 days. Toast bread. Top chickpea tuna sandwiches with arugula, tomato, onion, avocado, or add whatever you like!

ENTREES

Cauliflower Sheet Pan Fajitas

Prep Time: 10-15 minutes

Cook Time: 15-25 minutes

Ingredients

- •1 head of cauliflower chopped small
- 2 red peppers julienne
- 2 green peppers julienne
- 2 orange peppers julienne
- 1 yellow pepper julienne
- 1 red onion, julienne
- 2 tbsp grapeseed oil
- 1/8 tsp salt, or to taste
- 1 tbsp chili powder
- 1 tbsp cumin
- 2 tbsp paprika
- 2 tbsp smoked paprika
- 1 tbsp garlic powder
- 1 tsp onion powder
- 1 pack of tortillas

Instructions

1. Preheat oven to 425°F.
2. Spread oil onto a medium sheet pan. Cover in parchment paper.
3. Add all spices into a small bowl and mix. Set aside.
4. In a large bowl, mix chopped cauliflower, peppers, onions, spice mixture, salt and grapeseed oil.
5. Add the mixture to sheet pan(s) and roast for 15-25 minutes.
6. Heat tortilla according to packaging directions.
7. Serve tortillas alongside black or red beans and rice. Add guacamole, vegan sour cream, and Pico de Gallo.

Spaghetti Squash

Prep Time: 10-15 minutes

Cook Time: 30-45 minutes

Ingredients

- **1 medium spaghetti squash**
- **1 tbsp avocado oil**
- **1 pinch salt**
- **1 pinch pepper**

Instructions

1. Preheat oven to 350°F.
2. Cut squash in half. Gut the inside by removing all seeds and excess squash.
3. Season with salt and pepper and drizzle avocado oil.
4. Turn face down and cook for 30-45 minutes (depending on size of squash).
5. Remove squash from oven and turn face up. Let cool for 5-10 minutes.
6. Fork squash until squash has loosened from flesh; do not remove.
7. Leave squash in flesh and top with spaghetti or lemon butter (see sauces on pg. 82).

BBQ Jackfruit

Prep Time: 10-15 minutes

Cook Time: 15-25 minutes

Ingredients

- **2 canned Jackfruit in water**
- **1 tbsp liquid smoke**
- **1 tbsp Worcestershire sauce**
- **1 tbsp grapeseed oil**
- **1 green pepper**
- **1 red pepper**
- **1 vidalia onion**
- **1 tsp pepper**
- **1 tbsp chili powder**
- **½ cayenne pepper**
- **1 tbsp smoked paprika**
- **2 tbsp paprika**
- **1 tsp epis**
- **¼ cup bbq sauce**

Instructions

1. Drain jackfruit and remove any seeds and cut the ends off. Soak at least six hours or overnight in water. This removes the sticky residue.
2. Drain and dry very well. Season at least 4 hours prior to preparing.
3. Season jackfruit with liquid smoke, pepper, Worchester sauce, and paprika.
4. Preheat oven to 400°F.
5. Heat grapeseed oil on medium high in a cast iron skillet. Add jackfruit and cook for 10-15 mins. Pour excess liquid from bowl, add onions, peppers, and cook for 5 minutes.
6. Add BBQ sauce. Place in oven for 5-10 minutes.

7. Toast bun in toaster oven or flat side down in a skillet until golden brown.

8. Add jackfruit on flat side of bun top with avocado slaw. Place red bean on top of slaw or serve separately.

Spinach and Artichoke Paella

Prep Time: 10-15 minutes

Cook Time: 20-35 minutes

Ingredients

- **2 c jasmine basmati rice (you may use: brown, long grain, etc)**
- **1 tsp of ground turmeric**
- **1 tsp saffron**
- **2 tbsp of grapeseed oil**
- **2 cloves of garlic minced**
- **½ c of diced onion**
- **½ c of diced celery**
- **½ c of diced red bell pepper**
- **4 c of vegetable stock**
- **1 tsp of smoked paprika**
- **½ tsp of garlic powder**
- **½ tsp of onion powder**
- **1 can of Hearts of Palm Artichoke**
- **1 ½ c of fresh spinach whole**
- **Fresh lime and cilantro, to garnish**

Instructions

1. Heat the oil in a skillet. When the oil is hot, sauté the rice, turmeric, and saffron together for a few moments. Then, add in: garlic, onion, celery, and bell pepper; cook 2-3 minutes. Be sure to stir occasionally.
2. Add vegetable stock, smoked paprika, paprika, garlic powder, onion powder, artichoke palms, and fresh spinach. Stir well to combine.
3. Cook on medium heat until all the liquid evaporates.
4. Preheat the oven to 400°F. When liquid evaporates, throw the pan in the oven, cook for 5-7 minutes or until top and bottom of the rice is slightly crusty.
5. Garnish with fresh lime juice and cilantro and serve immediately.

Falafel Balls

Prep Time: 5-10 minutes

Cook Time: 20-30 minutes

Ingredients

- **2 cans of chickpeas (Garbanzo beans)**
- **5 garlic cloves**
- **1 Vidalia onion**
- **1 bunch of scallions**
- **1 green pepper**
- **1 red pepper**
- **1 tbsp epis**
- **2 tbsp all-purpose flour**
- **1 cup bread crumbs or crushed crackers**
- **2 tbsp cornstarch**
- **1 tsp cumin**
- **1 pinch pepper**
- **1 tbsp Mrs. Dash garlic and herb seasoning**
- **1 pinch salt**
- **2 c grapeseed oil (oil of choice)**
- **½ c parsley**
- **½ c cilantro**
- **½ thyme**

Instructions

1. In a food processer mix beans, parsley, cilantro, chopped onion, chopped green pepper, chopped red pepper, cumin, seasoning, salt, and. Mix until beans and peppers are dissolved.
2. Transfer mixture to a mixing bowl. Add 2 tbsp of flour and bread crumbs. Mix well.
3. Form dough into golf ball size falafels, coat with bread crumbs.
4. Heat canola oil in medium size pot. Drop balls once oil is very hot. Cook 2-3 minutes per side.

See Sides, Sauces and Salad (pages 81, 86 and 53)

Eggplant "Bakon" SLT (Spinach, Lettuce, Tomato)

Prep Time: 15-25 minutes

Cook Time: 10-15 minutes

Ingredients

- **2 slices of multi-grain or wheat bread**
- **1 tomato sliced**
- **½ c spinach**
- **½ Vidalia onion sliced**
- **sandwich pickle**

Instructions

1. Preheat oven to 275°F. Line baking sheet with parchment paper.

2. Slice eggplant in ½ inch lengthwise. Cut lengthwise again so you have four long skinny pieces.

3. Use a sharp knife or vegetable slicer to slice into very thin strips, resembling the appearance of bacon.

4. Use a brush or spoon to brush one side of the eggplant slice with sauce. Arrange in a single layer on the parchment paper lined baking sheet.

5. Bake for 15 minutes then flip over and brush remaining sauce over eggplant piece; bake 15 additional mins.

6. Toast two pieces of whole wheat or multi-grain slices of bread in toaster/ toaster over until brown.

7. Spread aioli, spinach, tomato, and sliced onion on one slice of bread. Cover the second piece of bread with aioli and lay four pieces of eggplant on bread. Slice sandwich in half and serve with sweet potato chips (See page 82 for recipe).

Marinade

Ingredients

- ½ tsp coconut amino
- 2 tsp liquid smoke
- 1 tsp Worcestershire sauce
- 1 tbsp cracked black pepper
- 1 tsp smoked paprika
- 1 tbsp maple syrup
- 1 pinch of onion powder
- 2 tbsp avocado oil

Instructions

1. In a small whisking bowl, whisk avocado oil, coconut amino, liquid smoke, Worcestershire sauce, maple syrup, smoked paprika, sea salt, onion powder, garlic, and black pepper. Set aside.

"Chick (Chana Masala)" N Grits

Prep Time: 5-10 minutes

Cook Time: 20-30 minutes

Chana

Ingredients

- 1 can or 2 c fresh garbanzos peas
- 2 tbsp red curry
- 2 tbsp of curry
- 2 tbsp garam masala
- 2 tbsp grapeseed oil
- ½ tbsp coriander
- 1 tbsp turmeric
- ½ tbsp saffron
- 1 green pepper diced
- 1 yellow pepper diced
- 1 orange pepper diced
- ½ vidalia onion diced
- ½ tsp of paprika diced
- dash pepper
- 2 tbsp fresh or dry thyme
- 2 tbsp tomato paste
- 2 tbsp grapeseed oil
- 1 tbsp coconut oil
- ½ c coconut milk
- ½ tsp cumin
- 2 c grapeseed oil (oil of choice)
- ½ c parsley
- ½ c cilantro
- ½ thyme

Instructions:

1. Drain and rinse chickpeas.
2. Heat grapeseed oil in a cast iron skillet, add one tbsp of red curry and simmer on medium-high 2 minutes.
3. Add cumin, one tbsp red curry, and yellow curry, cook for 10 minutes.

4. Add thyme, remaining red curry and garlic let cook for 2-3 minutes.

5. Add all herbs, onions, and peppers. Cook 5 minutes.

6. Add extra curry and seasoning for more color and flavor (optional).

7. Add tomato paste and ¾ cup of water cook 2-3 minutes.

8. Add coconut milk, cover, and cook for 15 minutes.

Yellow Corn Grits

Ingredients

- 1 c grits
- ½ c vegan milk
- ¼c c water
- 1 tbsp vegan butter
- dash salt
- dash pepper

Instructions

1. In a medium pot bring water to a boil, add milk, grits, and butter. Turn heat to low. Cover and cook for 30 minutes stirring occasionally. Add more milk until desired consistency is achieved.

2. Place in a bowl, top with sautéed spinach and tomato.

SIDES

Black Beans

Prep Time: 30-45 minutes

Crockpot: 6-8 hours

Stove Cook Time: 60-90 minutes

Ingredients

- **2 c of fresh black beans**
- **4 c of vegetable broth**
- **2 c water**
- **1 tbsp of coconut oil**
- **2 tbsp epis***
- **2 garlic cloves**
- **1 pinch of salt**
- **1 celery chopped**
- **1 carrot chopped**
- **½ yellow pepper**
- **½ red pepper**
- **½ green pepper**
- **½ onion**
- **1 pinch pepper**

Instructions

1. Soak beans in water for 2-3 hours.
2. Add all ingredients and seasoning in crock pot.
3. Cook in crock pot on high for 6-8 hours.

I hosted an intimate silent tasting for the cookbook. A good friend of mine invited her friend and daughter Zoey. Zoey is a three-year-old vibrant, intelligent, and most adorable little Queen. She entered with her purse and cute sundress; I felt underdressed. Other than the food, she was the star of the party. Zoey and I immediately hit it off with one another. She loved the lemon pound cake batter I allowed her to sample, the chocolate chip cookies, and the ginger water especially. She also is a water sponge and feel in love with the pool. She walked outside and took off her shoes without permission and stuck her feet in the pool; it was a challenge to get her from the pool after that. It turns out Zoey's favorite vegetable is Brussel sprouts. It was only right to name my favorite dish after Goddess Zoey.

Zoey's Roasted Brussies

Prep Time: 10-20 minutes

Cook Time: 15-25 minutes

Ingredients

- **1 lb. of brussels sprouts**
- **2 garlic cloves**
- **½ onion diced**
- **Pinch of salt**
- **Pinch of pepper**
- **1 tbsp balsamic (vinaigrette)**
- **½ tsp red wine vinegar**
- **1 tbsp grapeseed oil**
- **1 orange pepper diced**

Instructions

1. Preheat oven to 400°F.

2. In a cast iron skillet, heat avocado oil. Add Brussel sprouts, seasoning,

and onion.

3. Cook on medium heat for 10 mins.

4. Add balsamic vinegar and red wine vinegar.

5. Bake 10 minutes or until tender.

Rosemary Garlic Smashed Yuca

Prep Time: 10-20 minutes

Cook Time: 25-35 minutes

Ingredients

- **1 large yuca**
- **1 tbsp rosemary**
- **2 cloves of garlic**
- **1 c of water**
- **½ tsp vegan butter**

- **¼ c vegan milk**
- **¼ tsp salt**
- **¼ tsp pepper**
- **½ tsp rosemary**

Instructions

1. Cut yuca into quarter size pieces.

2. Add sliced yuca, onion, and garlic to boiling water. Cook for 20-30 mins until tender.

3. Drain yuca, transfer to pot and smash until there is a smooth consistency.

4. Add butter, milk, salt, pepper and rosemary.

Red Beans

Prep Time: 30-45 minutes

Cook Time: 60-90 minutes

Crockpot: 6-8 hours

Ingredients

- **2 c of fresh red beans**
- **4 c of vegetable broth**
- **4 garlic cloves**
- **¼ tsp salt**
- **½ onion diced**
- **¼ tsp pepper**
- **2 tbsp liquid smoke**
- **1 tbsp Worcestershire sauce**
- **1 tbsp turmeric**
- **½ tbsp saffron**
- **1 tsp cumin**

Instructions

1. Soak beans in water for 1-2 hours. Rinse well.
2. Add all ingredients in pot, cover and cook on medium high for two to three hours or until tender.

Crockpot:

1. Place all ingredients in crockpot.
2. Cook on high for at least four hours. Turn to low heat and cook for an additional two to four hours or until tender.

Red Cabbage Avocado Slaw

Prep Time: 10-15 minutes

Ingredients

- ½ head of purple cabbage shredded
- 1 carrot shredded
- 2 avocados diced
- ¼ c vegan mayo
- 1 pinch of salt
- ⅛ tsp pepper
- ½ lime juice

Instructions

1. Chop cabbage and dice avocado.
2. In a bowl mix cabbage, mayo, seasoning and lime juice. Gently fold in avocado.
3. Refrigerate for at least an hour or until ready to serve.

Cilantro Lime Rice

Prep Time: 5-10 minutes

Cook Time: 30-45 minutes

Ingredients

- **2 c Basmati Rice**
- **1 lime**
- **2 tbsp cilantro**
- **4 c vegetable broth**
- **2 tbsp grapeseed oil**
- **¼ tsp salt**
- **¼ tsp pepper**

Instructions

1. In a medium pot sauté garlic, onions and peppers. Add salt and pepper. Sauté until veggies are tender.

2. Add broth, taste and add seasoning to desired preference.

3. Adjust to high heat; once boiling add rice.

4. When water begins to recede, turn to low heat, cover with foil, and cook 25 minutes.

5. Uncover rice, gently fluff rice with fork. Drizzle grapeseed oil, lime juice, and cilantro.

SAUCES

Buffalo Sauce

Prep time: 5 mins

Cook time: 10

Total: 15 mins

Ingredients

- **1 bottle vegan Buffalo sauce**
- **1 tbsp vegan butter**
- **dash of cayenne pepper**
- **dash of red pepper flakes**

Instructions

1. In medium saucepan, heat buffalo sauce until bubbles form add butter.
2. Cook on medium-low heat for 10 minutes.

Sriracha Aioli

Prep time: 5 mins

Cook time: 0

Total: 5 mins

Ingredients

- **¼ Vegan mayo of choice**
- **1 tsp cilantro or parsley**
- **1 tsp lemon zest**
- **1 tsp sriracha**
- **½ tsp lemon juice**
- **1 tsp black pepper**
- **1 tsp paprika**
- **½ tsp smoked paprika**

Instructions

1. In a small bowl whisk mayo, sriracha, paprika, smoked paprika, garlic powder complete seasoning, lemon, and cilantro.

2. Stir until it is completely red. Add more seasoning and sriracha according to preference.

Balsamic Vinaigrette Dressing

Prep time: 5 mins

Marinade time: 10

Total: 15 mins

Ingredients

- 4 tbsp olive oil
- 2 tbsp balsamic vinegar
- 2 tbsp red wine vinegar
- 1 garlic clove
- 1 tsp onion powder
- 1 tsp black pepper
- 1 tsp smoked paprika
- dash of salt

Instructions

1. In a medium bowl whisk olive oil and red wine vinegar.
2. Combine herbs and spices, let sit for 10 minutes. Drizzle over salad.

Tomato Sauce

Prep time: 15 minutes

Cook time: 15 minutes

Total: 30 minutes

Ingredients

- 1 tbsp grapeseed oil
- 2 tomatoes
- 2 tbsp oregano
- 1 tsp saffron
- ½ tsp turmeric
- 1 c vidalia onion
- 1 c portobello mushrooms (optional)

- **dash of black pepper**
- **1 c green pepper**
- **1 c orange pepper**

Instructions

1. Preheat oven to 350°F.
2. Slice onion, green pepper, orange pepper, yellow pepper, mushrooms (optional) and tomato. Add pepper, turmeric, oregano, saffron, and salt, and garlic.
3. Place in glass baking pan.
4. Spread grapeseed oil evenly and bake 10-20 minutes or until vegetables are soft.
5. Drizzle with lemon juice and garnish with parsley.

Lemon Butter

Prep time: 5 minutes

Cook time: 10-15 minutes

Ingredients

- **1 lemon**
- **1 tbsp vegan butter**
- **½ c white wine (dry or cooking)**
- **½ c mushrooms (optional)**
- **1 c spinach**
- **2 tbsp grapeseed oil**
- **2 garlic cloves**
- **dash of salt**
- **dash of pepper**

Instructions

1. In a medium sauce pan, sauté garlic in grapeseed oil. Add mushrooms,

salt, and pepper. Cook until mushrooms are tender.

2. Add butter and spinach; cook for 2 minutes.

3. Turn heat to low and add white wine. Simmer for 10-15 minutes.

Tzatziki Sauce

Prep time: 5 minutes

Ingredients

- ½ cucumber
- ½ tbsp fresh dill
- ½ tsp lemon zest
- dash of salt
- ½ c plain vegan yogurt

- 2-4 garlic cloves
- 1 tbsp fresh lemon juice

Instructions

1. Grate the cucumber and place in cheese cloth to drain excess water.

2. Add cucumber, dill, salt, cashews, yogurt, lemon zest, garlic, and lemon to a food processor and pulse until smooth. Add more yogurt if sauce is too thick.

3. Refrigerate. Will last at least a week.

Epis

Haitian Epis is a flavor based used in nearly all Haitian food. The recipe varies from region to region and cook to cook, but it typically contains peppers, garlic, and various herbs. The base is commonly used to make rice and bean, stews, and soups. Epis originates from Taino and African roots; it is like Sofrito used in Hispanic cuisine. In many rural parts of Haiti, epis is created using wooden Mortar with pestle.

I was introduced to Epis and immediately fell in love with the freshness of the herbs. Epis reminds me of vegetable broth in seasoning form; the vegetables are based on your preference. When I smelled the flavors and tasted the freshness of the herbs and seasoning I knew it was a staple item to have in my kitchen. The great thing is there isn't a right or wrong way to make Epis. Epis is one of those items that doesn't really have an actual recipe or measurements! It's one of those recipes' grandma made with leftover vegetables and spices, then mom altered and put her twist, and lastly you added your top-quality herbs and spices. Based on who speak with, the ingredients will vary. Below is my version of traditional Haitian Epis. Feel free to add or omit ingredients based on your preference. Epis last several weeks frozen in a glass jar.

Haitian Epis

Prep Time: 15-25 minutes

Cook Time: 0

Ingredients

- 4 garlic cloves
- Orange Pepper
- Celery stalks
- 1 Yellow Pepper
- 1 Green Pepper
- Whole cloves or 1 tbsp clove powder
- 1 large vidalia onion
- Fresh thyme
- Scallion
- 1 bunch parsley
- 2 tbsp coconut oil
- Cilantro
- 2 tbsp white vinegar
- 1 scotch bonnet
- ¼ c grapeseed oil
- 1 cube vegetable bouillon

Instructions

1. Cut ingredients small enough to blend easily in a food processor.
2. Blend until smooth. Taste and add more herbs according to taste.
3. Store in a mason jar for up to 2 weeks.

DESSERTS

Chocolate Chip Cookies

Prep time: 10 mins

Cook: 10 mins

Total: 20 minutes

Ingredients

- **1 c of coconut oil or softened vegan butter**
- **½ c brown sugar**
- **½ c cane sugar**
- **¼ c vegan milk (I usually use almond)**
- **1 tsp vanilla bean or vanilla extract**
- **2 ½ c unbleached all-purpose flour**
- **1 tsp baking soda**
- **½ c vegan mini chocolate chips**

Instructions

1. Pre-heat oven to 350°F.
2. In a large mixing bowl, add coconut oil, brown sugar, and cane sugar until light and fluffy.
3. Add the milk and vanilla. Mix well. Scrape the bowl and mix for a few more seconds.
4. Add the flour and baking soda. Mix until most of the flour is gone and the dough has formed. Switching to a wooden spoon or spatula, scrape the bowl and mix the dough until all the flour is incorporated.
5. Stir in chocolate chips.
6. Even form dough using ice cream scoop onto a baking sheet lined with parchment paper. Make sure each scoop has enough chocolate chips and flatten slightly.

7. Bake in the oven for 8-10 minutes until the edges of the cookies begin to turn golden brown.

8. Remove parchment paper from the baking sheet and onto a wire rack to cool.

9. Once the cookies have cooled, serve with milk or nice cream (See page 97 for recipe).

Brenda's Lemon Supreme Pound Cake

My mother Brenda always made this perfect lemon cake, my non-vegan cake version was just as delicious. I knew I had to keep this cake in the family and recreate a vegan recipe of my mom's famous cake. The first time I made this cake it was perfect! I altered the recipe a few times, but the results were incomparable, so I went back to basics. The moistness, lemon flavor, and smell of the house while this cake is baking leaves me speechless. I imagined myself in my mother's kitchen as a little girl watching her make this cake. I look forward to creating the same memories with my children.

Prep Time: 30-45 minutes

Cook Time: 60 minutes

Cool Time: 60-90 minutes

Cake:

Ingredients

- **2 c unbleached all-purpose Flour**
- **1 box lemon instant pudding**
- **2 tbsp Baking Powder**
- **¼ tsp Salt**
- **2 tbsp Lemon Zest**
- **½ c coconut oil**
- **1½ c sugar**
- **1 c vegan milk, unsweetened**
- **4 tbsp lemon juice**
- **1 tsp Vanilla Extract**
- **¼ c unsweetened vegan yogurt**

Glaze

Ingredients

- **1 c powdered sugar**
- **1 tbsp lemon juice**

Instructions

1. Preheat oven to 350°F. Grease an 8-10-inch Bundt pan.

2. In a large bowl combine flour, baking powder, salt and lemon zest. Stir until combined and set aside.

3. In a separate large bowl beat together the vegan butter and sugar until well combined. Stir in almond milk, vanilla extract, lemon juice and yogurt.

4. Add the liquid mixture to flour mixture. Thoroughly combine.

5. Pour batter into greased Bundt pan. Bake for 50-55 minutes until cake is golden brown and a toothpick inserted in the center comes out clean.

6. Let cake cool for 60 minutes. Remove cake from Bundt pan.

7. Once cake is completely cooled, prepare the glaze. Stir lemon juice into powdered sugar. Once it forms a pourable glaze, pour over the middle of the cake. The glaze should run down each side of the cake. Cut & Serve!

Trail Mix

Prep time: 5 minutes

Ingredients

- 1 c dried cranberries
- 1 c golden raisins
- 1 c vegan mini chocolate chips
- ¼ c pistachios
- ¼ c walnuts
- ¼ c pecans

- ¼ c almonds
- ¼ c peanuts
- ¼ c dried roasted peanuts

Instructions

1. Mix all items in a medium bowl.
2. Package in snack size sandwich bags

Strawberry Sorbet

Prep Time: 30-45 minutes

Cook Time: 20 minutes

Freeze Time: 4-6 hours

Ingredients

- 2 ½ c fresh strawberries (previously frozen)
- 1 c water

- ¾ c sugar
- 1 tbsp lemon juice

Instructions

1. Let strawberries thaw until soft enough to blend; if using unfrozen berries be sure to wash and hull them.

2. Combine the water and sugar in a medium sized saucepan and stir until sugar is dissolved. Remove from heat. Let it cool to room temperature.

3. Place strawberries and syrup in food processor, process until smooth; do not puree'.

4. Add the syrup and lemon juice, and pulse briefly to combine. Strain mixture through a fine mesh strainer.

5. Place the mixture in a flat pan; an 8" x 8" or 9" round cake pan are both good choices. Place the pan in the freezer.

6. After 2 hours, use a fork or spoon to stir it around, bringing the frozen edges into the center. Return to the freezer.

7. Stir every hour or so, until the sorbet is nearly as firm as you like. This may take as little as 4 hours total, start to finish; or longer, depending on the temperature of your freezer.

One Ingredient Banana Nice Cream

Prep Time: 30-45 minutes

Cook Time: 60-90 minutes

Ingredients

- **4 frozen ripe bananas**

Instructions

1. Line a plate or baking sheet with parchment paper. Slice bananas into four equal parts and place on the paper evenly spaced. Freeze the banana pieces for a few hours up to overnight, or until firm.

2. Remove bananas from the freezer ad place them in a food processor.

3. When you're ready to prepare the nice cream, start by pulsing the frozen banana a few times until small crumbles form.

4. Continue processing. As you do so you'll notice the banana mixture clumping or sticking from time to time. Open the processor and use a spatula to spread the mixture out evenly throughout the processor so that it processes smoothly.

This is a basic recipe for basic banana soft serve, but it can easily be altered and improved by adding other ingredients such as: cocoa powder, other frozen fruits, vegan milk, etc

BONUS

Fruit Smoothie

Ingredients

- ¼ c strawberries
- ¼ c pineapple
- ¼ c kiwi
- ½ c pineapple gingerade

Instructions

1. Mix all ingredients in the blender.
2. Add water according to desired thickness.

Amaranth with maple syrup and nuts

Ingredients

- 2 c vegan milk
- 2 tbsp milk (use for garnish)
- 1 cinnamon stick grated of 1 tsp cinnamon
- 1 c amaranth
- 4 tbsp vegan butter
- ¼ c brown sugar
- 4 tbsp maple syrup
- ½ c walnuts

Instructions

1. In a medium saucepan bring the milk and water to a boil.
2. Whisk in the amaranth, reduce the heat to low and cover. Simmer for 30 minutes, stirring occasionally, until the liquid evaporates, and the amaranth is tender.
3. Remove the amaranth from the heat and stir in the butter, maple syr-

up, brown sugar and grated cinnamon.

4. Pour remaining milk and garnish with nuts of your choice. Serve warm.

Avocado Hummus

Prep Time: 0-5 minutes

Cook Time: 0-5 minutes

Ingredients

- **2 avocados**
- **1 tomato**
- **1 tbsp cilantro**

- **1 tbsp red onion**
- **¼ tsp salt**
- **¼ tsp pepper**

Hummus

Ingredients

- **1 c chickpeas**
- **1 tsp sriracha**

- **1 tbsp lime juice**
- **1 tbsp parsley**

Instructions

1. In a blender combine chickpeas, sriracha, parsley, and lime juice.

2. Slice avocados with knife or avocado slicer.

3. Place avocados on hummus, add tomatoes, salt, pepper, red onion, cilantro, and lime juice.

4. Garnish with mint.

Honey Mustard

Prep time: 5 minutes

Ingredients

- ¼ c of mayo
- ½ c of Dijon mustard
- ¼ c of olive oil
- 1 tbsp of grapeseed oil
- ¼ tsp salt
- ¼ tsp pepper

Instructions

1. Mix mayo, mustard, grapeseed oil, salt, and pepper with an emulsion blender.
2. Slowly drizzle in olive oil.
3. Refrigerate for at least 30 minutes.

Ranch

Prep time: 5 minutes

Ingredients

- 1 c of vegan mayo
- ½ tsp distilled vinegar
- 2 tbsp dill
- ½ tsp lemon
- ¼ tsp salt
- ¼ tsp pepper
- ½ tsp smoked paprika

Instructions

1. In a small bowl whisk mayo and vinegar, set aside for 5 minutes.
2. Add dill, garlic, salt, pepper, paprika, and lemon.

3. Mix all ingredients together, add more season to desired tasting.

4. Refrigerate overnight; it will last up to a week.

Simple Lime Dressing

Prep time: 5 mins

Cook time: 0

Total: 5 minutes

Ingredients

- **Juice of one lime**
- **½ tsp olive oil**

Instructions

1. Combine olive oil and lime juice with a spoon.

2. Drizzle on salad.

Balsamic Glazed Carrots

Prep Time: 10-20 minutes

Cook Time: 30-45 minutes

Ingredients

- ½ lb. carrots julienne
- ¼ tsp salt
- ¼ tsp pepper
- 1 tsp grapeseed oil
- 1 tbsp balsamic vinegar
- 4 tbsp brown sugar

Instructions

1. Heat oven to 350°F.

2. Slice carrots thinly (julienne) and wash thoroughly.

3. Pat dry with a paper towel. Place carrots on parchment paper.

4. Season with salt and pepper. Drizzle with grapeseed oil, brown sugar, and balsamic vinegar.

5. Bake for 30-45 minutes or until tender.

Roasted Red Cabbage with Carrots

Prep Time: 30-45 minutes

Cook Time: 60-90 minutes

Ingredients

- **1 head of red cabbage**
- **2 carrots diced**
- **1 vidalia onion**
- **1 tsp red pepper flakes**
- **1 tbsp balsamic vinegar**
- **½ tbsp red wine vinegar**
- **1 tbsp grapeseed oil**
- **¼ tsp salt**
- **¼ tsp pepper**

Instructions

1. Heat oven to 350°F.

2. Cut cabbage into four pieces. Slice cabbage thinly. Wash and drain.

3. In a cast iron skillet heat grapeseed oil. Add cabbage, carrots, red pepper flakes, salt, pepper, onion, and carrots. Cook 10-20 minutes. Add balsamic and red wine vinegar.

4. Place skillet in oven and bake 15 minutes.

"Meat"less Loaf

Prep Time: 10-20 minutes

Cook Time: 55-70 minutes

Ingredients

- 1lb portobello mushrooms (sliced)
- ½ celery diced or 2 tbsp celery seeds (add more depending on preference)
- 2 carrots diced
- ½ onion diced
- 2 tbsp avocado oil
- 2 tbsp all-purpose seasoning
- ½ red pepper diced
- ½ green pepper diced
- ½ yellow pepper diced
- 2 c rolled oats
- 1 tsp white vinegar
- 3 tbsp BBQ sauce
- 1 tbsp maple syrup
- ¼ tsp salt
- ¼ tsp pepper
- 1 tsp thyme
- 2 garlic cloves diced
- 1 c black beans
- 1 tbsp mustard
- ½ c red lentils
- ½ c bread crumbs or crushed crackers (optional)

Glaze

Ingredients

- 1 tbsp Mustard
- 2 tbsp BBQ sauce (of choice)
- 1 tbsp maple syrup
- 1 tsp parsley
- 1 tsp avocado oil

Instructions

1. Turn oven to 350°F.

2. Wash mushrooms. Pat dry with paper towel. Dice vegetables.

3. In a skillet heat avocado oil. Add celery, onion, carrots, peppers, garlic, thyme, all-purpose seasoning, salt, and pepper. Cook two minutes, add vinegar; cook three additional minutes. Put to the side.

4. In a blender or food processer add black beans and mushrooms and cooking oil. Puree for 2-3 minutes or until all blended.

5. Pour in medium bowl, add vegetables and oats. Mix with wooden spoon until all incorporated. Add BBQ sauce.

6. Place mixture in loaf pan and be sure to leave space around the edges so the glaze will leak down the sides of the pan.

7. Glaze loaf. Be sure to coat the edges.

8. Cook an hour. For added crisp, slice and heat each side in cast iron skillet (gives a nice crunch). Freeze leftover loaf for up to a month.

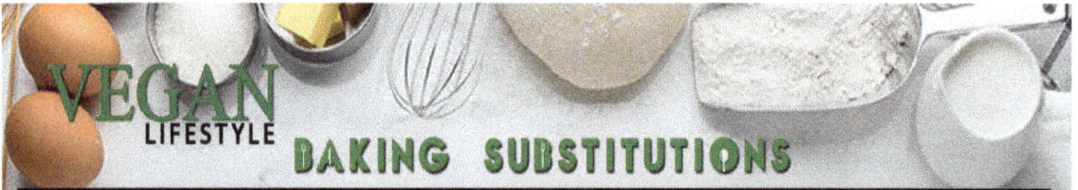

VEGAN LIFESTYLE

BAKING SUBSTITUTIONS

BUTTER/FAT

VEGAN BUTTER	COCONUT OIL	OLIVE OIL	APPLESAUCE	MARGARINE FULL FAT
SUBSTITUTE 1 FOR 1	SUBSTITUTE 1 FOR 1	1/4 C PLUS 2 TBSP FOR EVERY CUP OF BUTTER	1 TBSP PER EGG	SUBSTITUTE 1 FOR 1
ALWAYS READ LABELS	*ALWAYS READ LABELS*		*ALWAYS READ LABELS*	*ALWAYS READ LABELS*

MILK

CONDENSED MILK	BUTTERMILK	EVAPORATED MILK	CREAM	HEAVY CREAM
CANNED COCONUT MILK.	UNSWEETENED SOY MILK PLUS 2 TSP OF VINEGAR	UNSWEETENED COCONUT MILK	1 CUP: 3/4 CUP + 1 TBSP VEGAN MILK, PLUS 3 TBSP MELTED VEGAN BUTTER.	CAN OF COCONUT MILK CHILLED IN THE FRIDGE UP TO 48 HOURS; TOP LAYER REPLACES HEAVY CREAM.

EGG/EGG WHITE

AQUAFABA	BANANA	BAKING SODA & VINEGAR	GROUND FLAX OR CHIA SEED	PUREED TOFU
LIQUID FROM A CAN OF CHICKPEAS OR BLACK BEANS.	1 MASHED RIPE BANANA= 1 EGG	1 TSP BAKING SODA MIXED WITH 1 TBSP WHITE VINEGAR PER EGG (BAKING WAFFLES AND GOODS).	1 TBSP GROUND SEED AND 3 TBSP WATER PER EGG (BAKING BREAD).	1/4 CUP PUREED TOFU = 1 EGG (CUSTARD AND QUICHES)

SWEETENERS

AGAVE	MAPLE SYRUP	UNBLEACHED SUGAR	COCONUT CANE BROWN SUGAR

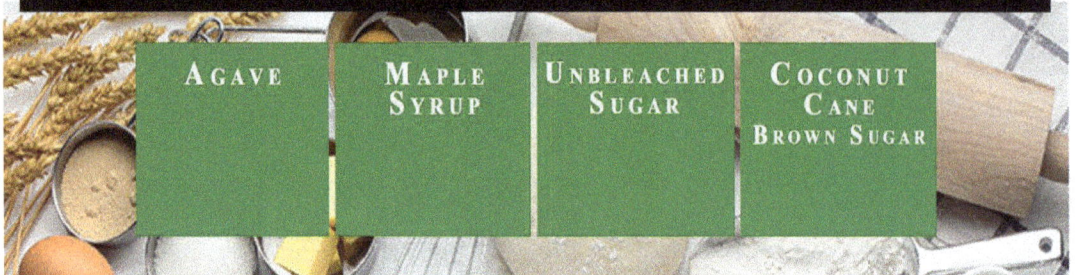

How To Cut Down a Recipe

Halve & Third Ingredients

Original	Half	One-Third
1 cup	1/2 cup	1/3 cup
3/4 cup	6 tbsp	1/4 cup
2/3 cup	1/3 cup	3 tbsp + 1-1/2 tsp
1/2 cup	1/4 cup	2 tbsp + 2 tsp
1/3 cup	2 tbsp + 2 tsp	1 tbsp + 1-1/4 tsp
1/4 cup	2 tbsp	1 tbsp + 1 tsp
1 tbsp	1-1/2 tsp	1 tsp
1 tsp	1/2 tsp	1/4 tsp
1/2 tsp	1/4 tsp	1/8 tsp
1/4 tsp	1/8 tsp	dash

VEGAN LIFESTYLE

Metric Table

United States method for measuring liquid and dry solid ingredients were used in this cookbook. The chart is to help cooks worldwide successfully master these recipes. Please note, all equivalents are approximate.

Equivalents for Liquid Ingredients by volume

tsp =	Tbsp =	cup =	fl oz =	ml
1/4 tsp =				1 ml
1/2 tsp =				2 ml
1 tsp =				5 ml
3 tsp =	1 Tbsp =		1/2 fl oz =	15 ml
	2 Tbsp =	1/8 cup =	1 fl oz =	30 ml
	4 Tbsp =	1/4 cup =	2 fl oz =	60 ml
	5 1/3 Tbsp =	1/3 cup =	3 fl oz =	80 ml
	8 Tbsp =	1/2 cup =	4 fl oz =	120 ml
	10 2/3 Tbsp =	2/3 cup =	5 fl oz =	160 ml
	12 Tbsp =	3/4 cup =	6 fl oz =	180 ml
	16 Tbsp =	1 cup =	8 fl oz =	240 ml
	1 pt =	2 cups =	16 fl oz =	480 ml
	1 qt =	4 cups =	32 fl oz =	960 ml

Oven Temperatures

Degrees Fahrenheit	Degrees Celsius
250	120
300	150
325	160
250	175
400	200

Dry Ingredients

Baking powder/soda	1 tsp	=	3 grams

Flour

All- purpose, unsifted	1 cup	120 grams
Cake or pastry, sifted	1 cup	100 grams
Whole wheat, unsifted	1 cup	125 grams
Nuts, coarsely chopped	1 cup	140 grams
Herbs, dry	1 tsp	2 grams
Rice uncooked	1 cup	5 grams
Salt	1 tsp	5 grams
Spices, ground	1 tsp	2 grams

Sugar

Granulated	1 tsp	5 grams
	1 tbsp	15 grams
Powdered	1 cup	110 grams
Brown (packed)	1 cup	220 grams

WEEKLY PLANNER

B-Breakfast / S-Snack / L-Lunch / D-Dinner / W-Water

MONDAY

B: Fruit Smoothie
S: Chocolate Chip Cookies
L: Red Beans
S: N/A
D: Spinach and Artichoke Paella
W: _____ oz. Pineapple Lemon Gingerade

TUESDAY

B: Toast
S: Small Portion Green Goddess Salad
L: Black Beans
S: Pico De Gallo
D: Jackfruit Tacos
S: Smoothie Bowl
W: _____ oz. Pineapple Lemon Gingerade

WEDNESDAY

B: Acorn Squash Boats
S: Guacamole
L: Lentil Soup
S: Fruit Salad
D: Cauliflower Fajitas
W: _____ oz. Purified Water

THURSDAY

B: Overnight Oats/Chia Pudding
S: Sweet Potato Chips
L: Cauliflower bites
S: Sautéed spinach and tomatoes
D: No "Meat"loaf with yuca and Balsamic Glazed Carrots
W: _____ oz. Purified Water

FRIDAY

B: Smoothie Bowl
S: Balsamic Glazed or Raw Carrots
L: Asparagus Salad
D: Eggplant "Bacon" Spinach and Tomato Sandwich with sweet potato chips
S: Strawberry Sorbet
W: _____ oz. Pineapple Lemon Gingerade & Purified Water

SATURDAY

B: Waffles
S: Strawberry Sorbet
L: Chickpea "Tuna" Salad
S: Trail Mix
D: Spaghetti Squash
S: Chocolate Chip Cookies
W: _____ oz. Purified Water

SUNDAY

B: Amaranth
S: Nuts
L: Veggie Broth
S: Chocolate chip cookies and Banana Nice Cream
D: Lentil Soup
W: _____ oz. Pineapple Lemon Gingerade & Purified Water

Please note on days with high carbs and starches snacks were omitted. Feel free to adjust.

SHOPPING LIST

Fruit, Ginger, Agave, Red/White Onion,

Coconut/Grape seed/Olive Oil, Sweet/White Potatoes, Rolled Oats,

Tomato, Spinach, Kale, Jalapeno, Avocado, Chia Seeds,

Cilantro, Parsley, Vegan Chocolate chips, Beans,

Tortillas, Carrots, Cauliflower, Jack fruit, Squash,

Asparagus, Cane Sugar, All-Purpose Flour, Amaranth, Nuts.

NOTES

Storage Containters

Mason Jars

*FOOD PREP *STAY FOCUSED!

WEEKLY PLANNER

VEGAN LIFESTYLE

MONDAY

TUESDAY

WEDNESDAY

THURSDAY

FRIDAY

SATURDAY

SUNDAY

SHOPPING LIST

_____
_____
_____
_____
_____
_____
_____
_____
_____
_____
_____
_____
_____
_____
_____
_____

NOTES

_____
_____
_____
_____
_____
_____

VEGAN
LIFESTYLE

MONTH _____   YEAR

Sunday	Monday	Tuesday	Wednesday	Thursday	Friday	Saturday

NOTES:

END OF MONTH CHECK

1. Current weight?

_____

2. Water intake?

_____

3. Mood?

_____

4. Energy level increase or decrease?

_____

5. Bowel movements?

    A. How frequent? _____

    B. Painful/bleeding/normal _____

    C. Hard or soft? _____

    D. Solid or balls? _____

6. Vitamins/Medication?

_____

7. Were my goals accomplished?

_____

Why Eating Fruit is Important

Fruit is high in vitamin C and antioxidants, which strengthens the immune system and wards off any invading bacteria and microbes.

The vitamins and minerals help your body function properly and can help prevent certain diseases and health conditions. Bananas, a common breakfast food, provide a good source of potassium, an important nutrient in muscle health.

Eating fruit for breakfast infuses the body with beneficial enzymes, fiber and prebiotics that help stimulate digestive juices in the stomach and push out old waste matter from the previous day.

Fruit fiber cleans the colon. Fruit in the morning is the best and natural way to gently awake the digestive system; large bowel movements are common.

PROTEIN SOURCES

There a broad variety of options, chia seeds are a great source of protein. According to 11 Proven Health benefits of Chia seeds by Kris Gunnars, BSc on August 8, 2018 (https://www.healthline.com/nutrition/11-proven-health-benefits-of-chia-seeds). Chia seeds are amongst the healthiest foods on the plant, 1oz (28) grams serving of chia seeds contains:

- Fiber: 11 grams.
- Protein: 4 grams.
- Fat: 9 grams (5 of which are omega-3s).
- Calcium: 18% of the RDI.
- Manganese: 30% of the RDI.
- Magnesium: 30% of the RDI.
- Phosphorus: 27% of the RDI.
- They also contain an impressive amount of zinc, vitamin B3 (niacin), potassium, vitamin B1 (thiamine) and vitamin B2.

Hemp Seeds

Hemp seeds are a part of the cannabis family. Yes, you heard correct! Hemp seeds are basically the cousin to marijuana, but the benefits are completely different. Hemp has low THC, easy to grow, and adjustable to most weather. This means you can easily grow this at home.

Hemp is used in food, body care, and automobiles (https://ministry-ofhemp.com/hemp/not-marijuana/). Hemp is placed in the cannabis family because of the misconceptions during the 1970's when President Nixon declared a "War on Drugs" and signed into law the Controlled Substances Act of 1970. This, unfortunately, classified hemp as a drug even though it doesn't include any of the chemicals that make marijuana a drug, which led to the extinction of hemp (https://ministryofhemp.com/hemp/not-marijuana/). About 25% of calories in hemp seeds come from protein, which is relatively high (https://www.healthline.com/nutrition/6-health-benefits-of-hemp-seeds#section4).

Hemp seeds provide amounts of protein like beef and lamb. Wait, it gets better, they are considered a whole protein source, meaning they provide all the necessary amino acids. Necessary amino acids are not made in the body and need to be obtained from the diet.

Almonds

Almonds are delicious and can be used in several ways: flour, garnish, milk, or even on a salad. I love to crush them up and garnish them on my favorite vegan chocolate chip cookie recipe (desserts tab). According to Joseph Nordqvist, "almonds are packed with vitamins, minerals, protein, and fiber, and are associated with several health benefits. Just a handful of almonds (approximately one ounce) contains one eighth of our daily protein needs. "The Health benefits of Almonds".

EGGPLANT BACON

CARROT BACON

SHIITAKE MUSHROOM BACON

COCONUT BACON

ZUCCHINI BACON

TEMPH BACON

RAW JICAMA BACON

INDEX

Lentils

Maple

Mango

Milk

Mist

Mushroom

Noodle

Nuts

Oil

  Avocado

  Coconut

  Grapeseed

Pasta

 Pepper

   Black, green, orange,

   red, yellow

Pico

Pineapple

Red Cabbage

Onion

Pepper

Rice

Cilantro lime

Salad

Salsa

Salt

Saffron

Sandwhich

Seasoning

Soup

Squash

Sugar

Toast

Tomato

Tumeric

Vanilla bean

Essence

Vinegar

Waffles

Yuca

BIBLIOGRAPHY:

Bjarnadottir, Adda MS (2017). *Six Evidence-Based Health Bene-fits of Hemp Seeds*. Retrieved   from https://www.healthline.com/nutri-tion/6-health-benefits-of-hemp-seeds#section4.

Gunnars, K. BSc (2018, August 8). *11 Proven Health benefits of Chia Seeds*. Retrieved from   https://www.healthline.com/nutrition/11-prov-en-health-benefits-of-chia-seeds.

https://www.dictionary.com

https://www.fitneass.com/fruit-for-breakfast-5-benefits/

https://livelovefruit.com/eating-fruit-for-breakfast-completely-trans-form-your-health/

https://ministryofhemp.com/hemp/not-marijuana/

www.ingramcontent.com/pod-product-compliance
Lightning Source LLC
Chambersburg PA
CBHW040254100426
42811CB00011B/1264